BLACK SHIPS

BLACK SHIPS

ILLUSTRATED JAPANESE HISTORY —THE AMERICANS ARRIVE

SEAN MICHAEL WILSON

ILLUSTRATIONS BY

AKIKO SHIMOJIMA

North Atlantic Books
Berkeley, California

Published by
North Atlantic Books
Berkeley, California

Cover design by Jasmine Hromjak
Interior design and artwork by Akiko Shimojima
Printed in the United States of America

Thanks to Davide Calzetti for his support with Japanese historical information.

Black Ships: Illustrated Japanese History—The Americans Arrive is sponsored and published by the Society for the Study of Native Arts and Sciences (dba North Atlantic Books), an educational nonprofit based in Berkeley, California, that collaborates with partners to develop cross-cultural perspectives, nurture holistic views of art, science, the humanities, and healing, and seed personal and global transformation by publishing work on the relationship of body, spirit, and nature.

North Atlantic Books' publications are available through most bookstores. For further information, visit our website at www.northatlanticbooks.com or call 800-733-3000.

Library of Congress Cataloguing-in-Publication data is available
from the publisher upon request.

1 2 3 4 5 6 7 8 9 United 22 21 20 19 18 17

North Atlantic Books is committed to the protection of
our environment. We partner with FSC-certified printers using
soy-based inks and print on recycled paper whenever possible.

AUTHOR'S PREFACE

Our goal with *Black Ships,* as with all the Japanese history, samurai, and martial arts books that we have done—thirteen of them so far—can be summarized as combining two aspects: accuracy and accessibility. We want to make books that make history more accessible as well as easier to enjoy and take in, and to do it via the mix of visuals and text that make comic books and manga special. It is regrettable that many of us, especially younger readers, have little knowledge of our own histories. In Japan this is particularly true, with people in their twenties knowing very little about the history of their own country. They often think of history as boring and difficult.

For these young people in Japan, and also in the United States, Britain, and other countries, I have this to say: history is interesting, and history is easy. It's not all about memorizing meaningless dates. If that is how it is being taught to you, then your educational system needs to change. History is about you; it is about your father, your grandmother, and your friends. It's about what those individuals struggled against, and how the things that surround you got to be that way. It's about how people used to live, what places used to look like. It's about the ghosts of yesterday who once walked the streets of today. It's also about learning lessons from our past so that we don't have to make the same mistakes.

In a world of growing conflict among various countries, systems, and religions, having a knowledge of history helps us be smarter, make better decisions, and avoid wars.

History is made up of engaging stories of fascinating characters, powerful movements, and events both large and small. Using a graphic format can help bring these stories to life, through combining an interesting narrative with drawings that help us visualize this pivotal period of Japanese history. Akiko Shimojima and I have thoroughly researched not only the events described in this story, but also the way the clothes, the guns, and the buildings would have looked; the way people then may have talked to each other; their gestures and movements. These books normally take about a year to make. From the first stage of research through writing the script, rough-sketching the art, inking, lettering, and going over it all for errors, these books normally take a year or more to make. It's a lot of work, but it's worth it, and it's something to be proud of. It is work that is worth getting up in the morning for.

This book starts in 1853 with the arrival of American ships in Japan, although it also steps back in time to explain some of the relevant history of the previous thirty-odd years. It takes us through the tense events of the negotiations between the Americans and Japanese and and the cultural clash that led to the famed "opening" of Japan, a period that is generally considered to have ended around 1860. We are currently working on our next book of Illustrated Japanese History: *The Satsuma Rebellion,* often called the last stand of the samurai. If you want to know more after reading *Black Ships,* this forthcoming volume will fill in more details of the last years of the Shogunate in the 1860s, the establishment of the Meiji government, and the rebellion of 1877.

There are many more stories to tell, of course. And remember: history is interesting, history is easy—and history is important.

—Seán Michael Wilson, Kumamoto, Japan

CHAPTER 1

KEH KEH KEH
WHAT IS THIS?
KEH KEH

KEH
Splash
KEH
KEH
KEH
Splash
IS IT A SEA DRAGON?
KEH
HOLD ON TO SOMETHING!
Splash
Splash
Splash
KEH
KEH
KEH

IN MAY 1853 THE AMERICAN SHIPS *PLYMOUTH*, *MISSISSIPPI*, *SARATOGA*, AND *SUSQUEHANNA* ARRIVED AT THE RYUKYU ISLANDS.

THE BLACK SHIPS
HAD ARRIVED...

IN THE 1830S AND 1840S EUROPEAN POWERS WERE INCREASINGLY STRUTTING IN AN AGGRESSIVE FASHION IN THE FAR EAST. CHINA LOST THE OPIUM WAR WITH BRITAIN AND IN THE 1842 TREATY OF NANKING WAS FORCED TO ACCEPT FREE TRADE AGREEMENTS THAT GAVE MUCH POWER TO WESTERN COUNTRIES.

BOOKS BY THE CHINESE WRITER WEI YUAN ABOUT THE POWER OF MARITIME COUNTRIES AND THE WEAKNESS OF CHINA WERE CIRCULATED AMONG A SMALL GROUP OF SCHOLARS AND FIGURES IN THE BAKUFU (THE SHOGUN'S OFFICE OR ADMINISTRATION). MINETO FUKO'S 1849 BOOK *KAIGAI SHINWA* (STORIES FROM ABROAD) SPREAD THESE CONCERNS TO MANY OTHERS.
THE AUTHORITIES CONSULTED THE ONLY FOREIGNERS THEY HAD ALLOWED LIMITED ENTRY TO IN NAGASAKI: THE DUTCH.
WHY HAVE THE CHINESE LOST? THEY SEEM BRAVE ENOUGH.
BRAVERY ALONE IS NOT ENOUGH. THE MODERN ART OF WAR DEMANDS SOMETHING MORE. NO OUTLANDISH POWER CAN COMPETE WITH A EUROPEAN ONE. AS YOU SEE, CHINA HAS BEEN CONQUERED BY ONLY FOUR THOUSAND MEN.
THE SHOGUNATE THEREFORE ALTERED THE EDICT DECISION BANNING FOREIGNERS TO ALLOW SOME TO BE HELPED IF BAD WEATHER FORCED THEM TO JAPAN. EVEN STILL, IT INSTRUCTED LOCAL DAIMYO LORDS:
"IF, HOWEVER, AFTER RECEIVING SUPPLIES, THEY DO NOT WITHDRAW, YOU WILL DRIVE THEM AWAY...
ADOPTING SUCH MEASURES AS ARE NEEDED."

IN 1844 KING WILLIAM ?? OF THE NETHERLANDS WROTE A POLITE LETTER TO THE SHOGUN, SUGGESTING A MORE OPEN POLICY:
DISTANCE IS BEING OVERCOME BY THE INVENTION OF THE STEAMSHIP. A NATION THAT TRIES TO HOLD ITSELF ALOOF FROM THIS PROCESS RISKS THE ENMITY OF OTHERS…
WHEN ANCIENT LAWS, BY STRICT CONSTRUCTION, THREATEN THE PEACE, WISDOM DIRECTS THAT THEY BE SOFTENED.
THE DUTCH WERE TOLD THAT THIS WAS IMPOSSIBLE, AND PLEASE DON'T WRITE AGAIN…
THERE WAS GREAT DISAGREEMENT ABOUT HOW TO REACT TO THE GROWING THREAT FROM THE FOREIGNERS AMONG THE BAKUFU, THE EMPEROR'S COURT, SCHOLARS, DAIMYO, AND SAMURAI.
IN 1846 THE UNITED STATES SENT CAPTAIN JAMES BIDDLE TO JAPAN, BUT IN EDO BAY HE WAS TOLD TO GO TO NAGASAKI, LIKE ALL THE REST. HE WAS MANHANDLED BY A GUARD WITHOUT REGISTERING MUCH COMPLAINT. THIS SEEMED TO SHOW THAT STRONG RESISTANCE TO THE FOREIGNERS MIGHT BE THE BEST POLICY.
THE AMERICANS SHIPS WITHDREW… THIS TIME!

BUT COMMODORE PERRY CAME IN WITH GREATER STRENGTH AND WITH A DETERMINATION TO SUCCEED.

BUCHANAN, PLEASE REPORT ON THE STATE OF THE MEN.
THREE MEN SICK HERE ON THE SUSQUEHANNA, COMMODORE PERRY, SIR.
THREE ALSO ON THE MISSISSIPPI, TWO ON THE PLYMOUTH, WITH SIXTEEN SICK ON THE SARATOGA.
SIXTEEN? WHAT HAPPENED THERE?
POSSIBLE FOOD POISONING, SIR, WHILE ON SHORE LEAVE IN HONG KONG.
ARRANGE A COMPANY OF A HUNDRED MARINES FROM THE PLYMOUTH TO JOIN ANOTHER HUNDRED HERE ON THE SUSQUEHANNA.
WE'LL GO ASHORE IN STRENGTH.

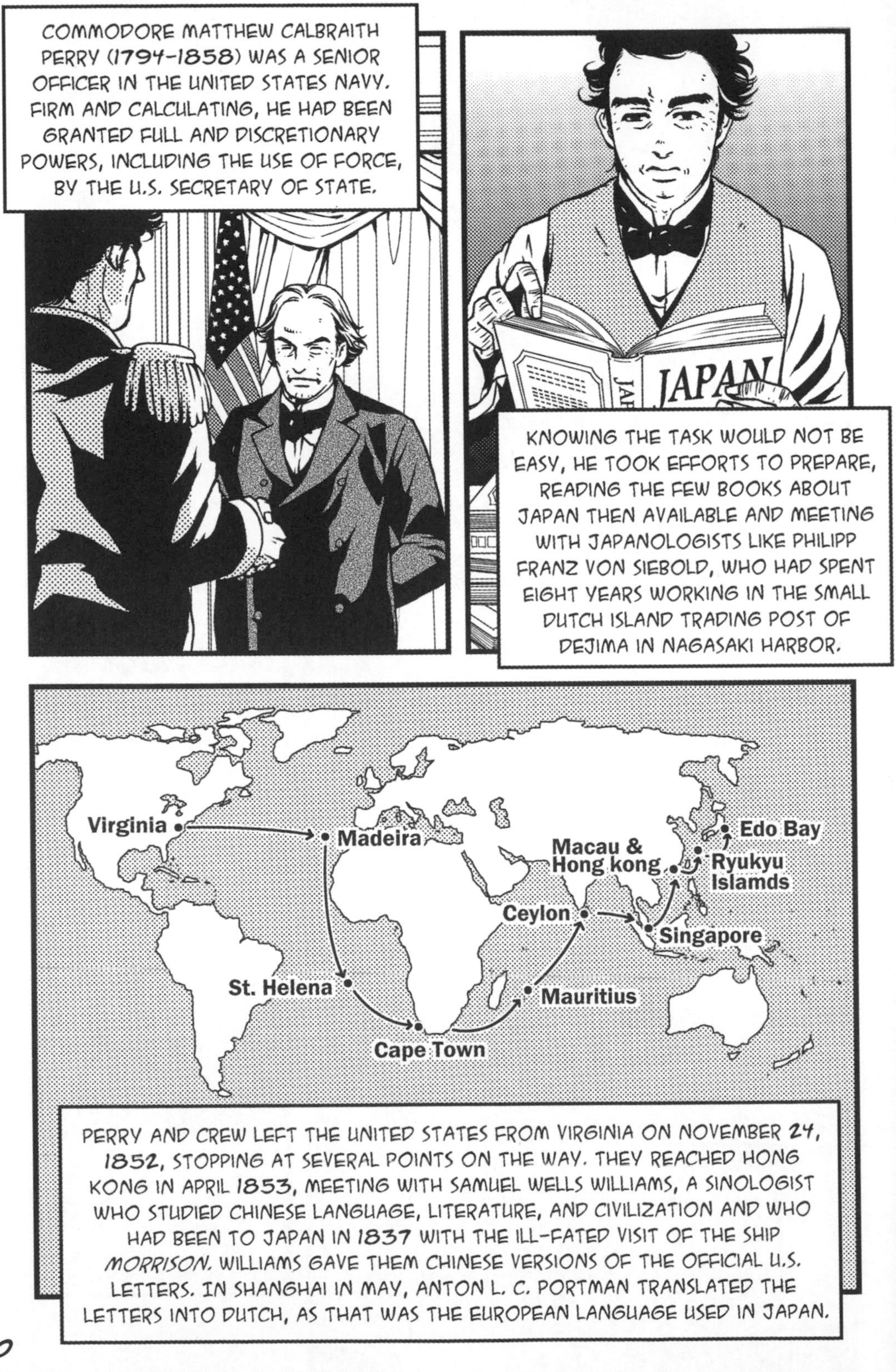

COMMODORE MATTHEW CALBRAITH PERRY (1794–1858) WAS A SENIOR OFFICER IN THE UNITED STATES NAVY. FIRM AND CALCULATING, HE HAD BEEN GRANTED FULL AND DISCRETIONARY POWERS, INCLUDING THE USE OF FORCE, BY THE U.S. SECRETARY OF STATE.

JAPAN

KNOWING THE TASK WOULD NOT BE EASY, HE TOOK EFFORTS TO PREPARE, READING THE FEW BOOKS ABOUT JAPAN THEN AVAILABLE AND MEETING WITH JAPANOLOGISTS LIKE PHILIPP FRANZ VON SIEBOLD, WHO HAD SPENT EIGHT YEARS WORKING IN THE SMALL DUTCH ISLAND TRADING POST OF DEJIMA IN NAGASAKI HARBOR.

Virginia
Madeira
St. Helena
Cape Town
Mauritius
Ceylon
Singapore
Macau & Hong kong
Ryukyu Islamds
Edo Bay

PERRY AND CREW LEFT THE UNITED STATES FROM VIRGINIA ON NOVEMBER 24, 1852, STOPPING AT SEVERAL POINTS ON THE WAY. THEY REACHED HONG KONG IN APRIL 1853, MEETING WITH SAMUEL WELLS WILLIAMS, A SINOLOGIST WHO STUDIED CHINESE LANGUAGE, LITERATURE, AND CIVILIZATION AND WHO HAD BEEN TO JAPAN IN 1837 WITH THE ILL-FATED VISIT OF THE SHIP *MORRISON*. WILLIAMS GAVE THEM CHINESE VERSIONS OF THE OFFICIAL U.S. LETTERS. IN SHANGHAI IN MAY, ANTON L. C. PORTMAN TRANSLATED THE LETTERS INTO DUTCH, AS THAT WAS THE EUROPEAN LANGUAGE USED IN JAPAN.

PERRY, NOW ON BOARD THE SUSQUEHANNA, CALLED ON THE RYUKYU ISLANDS, UNDER THE CONTROL OF THE SATSUMA DOMAIN OF JAPAN, FROM MAY 17 TO 26.
PERRY DRILLED HIS MARINES ON THE BEACH FOR HOURS AT A TIME IN A SHOW OF FORCE AND MILITARY CEREMONY DESIGNED TO IMPRESS THE ISLANDERS.

TELL THEM I REFUSE TO DEAL WITH LOCAL LEADERS.
I DEMAND AN AUDIENCE WITH THE HIGH OFFICIALS OF KING SHO TAI AT SHURI CASTLE.
PERRY HAD DECIDED THAT IN THIS LAND OF STRICT CEREMONY AND HIERARCHY, THE BEST POLICY WAS TO REMAIN ALOOF AND APPEAR TO BE AN UNQUESTIONABLY IMPORTANT FIGURE.
IT APPEARS TO HAVE WORKED, AS EVENTUALLY A MEETING WAS ARRANGED.

THE ACTUAL TALKS WERE A LONG AND DRAWN-OUT AFFAIR, AS PERRY KNEW NO JAPANESE AND THERE WERE ALMOST NO FLUENT ENGLISH SPEAKERS IN JAPAN. THEY USED DUTCH FOR SPOKEN CONVERSATIONS AND CHINESE FOR WRITTEN ("BRUSH") COMMUNICATION AND SOME DOCUMENTS.
WE PRESENT YOU WITH THE OFFICIAL DOCUMENTS FROM THE UNITED STATES GOVERNMENT…
PERRY'S WORDS WERE TRANSLATED INTO DUTCH BY WILLIAMS…
HIERBIJ PRESENTEREN WIJ DE OFFICIELE DOCUMENTEN NAMENS DE REGERING VAN DE VERENIGDE STATEN VAN AMERIKA.
THEN TRANSLATED FROM DUTCH TO JAPANESE…
アメリカ政府からの公文書をあなた方にお渡ししよう
THEN VICE VERSA: JAPANESE TO DUTCH TO ENGLISH!
えと…‘ありがとございます’
HARTELIJK DANK.
HE SAYS "THANK YOU VERY MUCH"… BUT SEEMS HESITANT TO TAKE THE LETTERS.

LATER, THE HIGH OFFICIALS WERE INVITED ABOARD THE SHIP.
GIVE THEM EVERY HOSPITALITY WHEN ONBOARD, ADAMS...
WE WILL WIN THEM OVER BY A MIXTURE OF FORCE, CEREMONY, AND A DISPLAY OF WEALTH.
LET'S HAVE THE FULL WORKS, MEN. PRETEND YOU'RE ON PARADE IN THE BARRACKS AT WASHINGTON. LOOK SHARP!

THE NEGOTIATIONS CONTINUED THERE, WITH PERRY CONTINUING TO PRESS AGGRESSIVELY.
WE DEMAND SUPPLIES, TRADING RIGHTS, AND LAND FOR A COALING STATION.
IF WE ARE REFUSED, THEN HAVE NO DOUBT THAT WE WILL ATTACK.
ALL THIS WAS CALCULATED TO HAVE A STRONG EFFECT WHEN NEWS OF IT REACHED THE SHOGUNATE IN EDO.
THEY APPEAR TO BE IN FEAR OF SOMETHING. I FANCY THAT IT IS NOT JUST OUR PRESENCE...
BUT A FEAR THEY HAVE OF THE TYRANNICAL RULE THEY SUFFER FROM THE MAINLAND.
POSSIBLY. IT'S HARD TO BE SURE.
IF SO, THE RYUKYU ISLANDS MAY WELCOME OUR LIBERATING THEM, TAKING THEM UNDER AMERICAN GUIDANCE.
I MAY RECOMMEND THIS WHEN WE GET BACK TO THE UNITED STATES.

THEY REQUEST THAT, LIKE ALL THE REST OF THE FOREIGNERS, WE GO TO NAGASAKI.
THEN TELL HIM THAT WE WILL NOT CONFINE OURSELVES TO NAGASAKI, "LIKE ALL THE REST."
I HAVE ORDERS TO DELIVER A LETTER FROM THE PRESIDENT OF THE UNITED STATES TO THE EMPEROR OF JAPAN.
AND THAT IS WHAT I WILL DO.

THIS IS A VERY DISTRESSING SITUATION. WHAT SHOULD WE DO?
WE COULD TRY TO EXPEL THEM BY FORCE, MY LORD.
THE 1825 EDICT COMMANDS THAT.
HMM... I DOUBT THAT WOULD MEET WITH SUCCESS.
WE NEED TO INFORM THE SHOGUN. IT IS THEIR RESPONSIBILITY TO PROTECT US.
THEY DEMAND ENOUGH FROM US; NOW THEY NEED TO PROVE THEIR SIDE OF THE SO-CALLED BARGAIN.

THERE HAD BEEN INCREASING CONTACT AND PRESSURE FROM THE "FOREIGN BARBARIANS" OVER THE LAST FIFTY YEARS.

IN 1804, DURING THE NAPOLEONIC WARS, A RUSSIAN EXPEDITION COMMANDED BY NIKOLAI REZANOV ENTERED NAGASAKI HARBOR, CARRYING A LETTER FROM CZAR ALEXANDER I ASKING FOR TRADE PRIVILEGES. THE BAKAFU MADE HIM WAIT FOR SIX MONTHS, THEN GAVE IT TO HIM STRAIGHT: NO!

ANGRY AT THIS, HE LATER SENT RAIDING PARTIES ASHORE AT SAKHALINM, AND IN 1811 THE JAPANESE CAPTURED A RUSSIAN SHIP AND HELD ITS CAPTAIN PRISONER FOR TWO YEARS.

BUT HE WAS SOON TREATED WITH MORE RESPECT, AND EVEN STARTED TO TEACH HIS HOSTS ABOUT MATHEMATICS AND ASTRONOMY.
IN 1808 THOMAS STANDFORD RAFFLES, FAMOUS FOR ESTABLISHING SINGAPORE, SENT A BRITISH SHIP, THE PHAETON, TO NAGASAKI. AT THE TIME THE DUTCH WERE IN A BIG MESS, HAVING BEEN OVERRUN BY NAPOLEON AT HOME IN THE NETHERLANDS, BUT WERE TRYING TO HIDE THIS FROM THE JAPANESE.

THE NAGASAKI OFFICIAL COMMITTED SEPPUKU AT THE DISGRACE OF LETTING FOREIGNERS OVERRUN HIS AREA. THE DISORDER OF THE DUTCH BECAME CLEAR TO THE BAKUFU IN EDO.

AS THE CLOTHES AND SHIPS OF THE VARIOUS NATIONALITIES LOOKED VERY SIMILAR TO THE JAPANESE, SOME FELT IT WAS ACTUALLY ONE SUPERPOWER THREATENING THEM, JUST PRETENDING TO COME FROM DIFFERENT AREAS.
SO, IN 1825 THE BAKUFU ISSUED AN EDICT THAT ALL FOREIGNERS WERE TO BE TREATED THE SAME:
ALL SOUTHERN BARBARIANS AND WESTERNERS WORSHIP CHRISTIANITY, THAT WICKED CULT PROHIBITED IN OUR LAND.
HENCEFORTH, WHENEVER A FOREIGN SHIP IS SIGHTED… ALL SHOULD FIRE ON IT AND DRIVE IT OFF…
HAVE NO COMPUNCTIONS ABOUT FIRING ON A DUTCH SHIP BY MISTAKE. WHEN IN DOUBT, DRIVE THE SHIP AWAY.
IF THE FOREIGNERS FORCE THEIR WAY ASHORE, YOU MAY CAPTURE THEM… IF THEIR MOTHER SHIP APPROACHES, YOU MAY DESTROY IT…

BUT, IN THE 1830S AND 1840S, FOREIGN SHIPS CAME ASHORE SEVERAL TIMES, INCLUDING A FRENCH SHIP AT NAHA IN OKINAWA, AND THE 1838 VISIT OF THE MORRISON, MENTIONED BEFORE.
EVEN THOUGH IT CONTAINED SEVEN SHIPWRECKED JAPANESE CITIZENS, IT WAS FIRED UPON BY THE GUNS AT EDO, AND AGAIN AT KAGOSHIMA.
SPLASH!
THESE FOREIGNERS ARE LIKE FLIES AROUND A BOWL…
RAVENOUS BEASTS!
FIRE AT THEM AGAIN!

AT THE SAME TIME, THE BAKUFU SECRETLY EMPLOYED VARIOUS SCHOLARS, CALLED THE BANSHA, TO STUDY WESTERN KNOWLEDGE.
AN INTERNAL DEBATE HAD ARISEN, WITH ONE KEY QUESTION: HOW SHOULD WE REACT TO THESE FOREIGNERS?
WATANABE KAZAN (1793-1841) WAS A KEY FIGURE. HE ARGUED THAT USING VIOLENCE AGAINST THE GREATER POWER OF THE WEST COULD LEAD TO DISASTER.
YOU MAY CALL THEM BARBARIANS... BUT THEY WILL NOT RESORT TO ARMS WITHOUT AN EXCUSE.
FOR HIS RADICAL VIEWS, HE WAS DENOUNCED AND CONVICTED. HE COMMITTED SEPPUKU TO SPARE HIS LORD ANY MORE TROUBLE.
TAKANO CHOEI, A STUDENT OF SIEBOLD'S, VOICED SIMILAR VIEWS AND WAS IMPRISONED FOR THEM. BUT HE ESCAPED.
SUGITA GENPAKU, A DUTCH TRANSLATOR, SEEING THE TROUBLE THAT OPEN VIEWS COULD GET HIM INTO, HELD HIMSELF IN CHECK. BUT WHEN HE WAS DRUNK, HE COULD NOT HELP BUT SHOUT OUT A DUTCH WORD HE HAD BECOME ENTRANCED WITH: FREEDOM!
VRIJHEIT!
VRIJHEIT!

ON THE OTHER HAND, THE MITO CLAN RETAINER, AIZAWA SEISHISAI, VOICED A TYPE OF JAPANESE ARROGANCE ALSO PRESENT AT THE TIME:
THE DIVINE REALM OF JAPAN IS RIGHTLY THE HEAD AND SHOULDERS OF THE WORLD AND CONTROLS ALL NATIONS.
THESE BARBARIANS, UNMINDFUL OF THEIR BASE POSITION, HAVE SCURRIED ACROSS THE WORLD AND NOW AUDACIOUSLY CHALLENGE US.
WHAT INSOLENCE!
SUCH PEOPLE WANTED A SIMPLE REACTION: ATTACK, DEFEAT, REPEL!

IN JULY 1853, THE BLACK SHIPS SET SAIL FOR MAINLAND JAPAN…
WHY ARE THE BRITISH NOT PRESSING JAPAN MORE?
SURELY WITH THEIR DOMINANCE IN CHINA THEY ARE IN A BETTER POSITION THAN US?
I HEARD FROM A BRITISH OFFICER IN HONG KONG THAT THE, UH… UNPLEASANTNESS OF THE RECENT WAR IN CHINA HAS MADE THEM HESITANT TO FORCE THINGS IN JAPAN.
AH HA. THAT IS PROBABLY WISE.
ALSO, FRANKLY, THEY CONSIDER THE TRADE PROSPECTS IN JAPAN TO BE RATHER SLIGHT.
HMM… THAT IS A MISTAKE, I THINK.
FROM THE LITTLE I HAVE LEARNED ABOUT THE JAPANESE IN MY STUDIES, IT SEEMS THAT THEY COULD BE A VERY INDUSTRIOUS PEOPLE.
SIEBOLD CERTAINLY THOUGHT SO.
"RIGHT UP UNTIL THEY KICKED HIM OUT!"

BEFORE SAILING TO EDO, THE CHINESE INTERPRETER, SIEH, DIED. PERRY'S JOURNAL: "AT ONE O'CLOCK THIS MORNING THE OLD CHINAMAN BREATHED HIS LAST, AGED FIFTY-FIVE YEARS. THOUGH AN EDUCATED MAN, EMPLOYED TO TEACH CHINESE TO FOREIGNERS..."
"HE HAD FOR MANY YEARS BEEN AN INVETERATE OPIUM SMOKER, AND HIS FRAME HAD BECOME SO WEAK THAT EVERYONE PREDICTED HE COULD NOT LONG SURVIVE."
THUS WE ARE LEFT WITHOUT A CHINESE INTERPRETER, FOR THOUGH MR. WILLIAMS CAN CONVEY THE MEANING OF ENGLISH WORDS INTO THE MANDARIN DIALECT, HE CANNOT HIMSELF WRITE IN THE MANDARIN OR THE JAPANESE LANGUAGE.
I HAD NEVER LEARNED MUCH MORE JAPANESE THAN WAS NECESSARY TO SPEAK WITH IGNORANT SAILORS...
AND THAT WAS NEARLY NINE YEARS AGO.

SO, A NEW TRANSLATOR JOINED THEM, LUO SEN XIANGQIAO (向喬, 1821–CA. 1899) FROM GUANGDONG PROVINCE. A REFINED MAN—AND NOT AN OPIUM SMOKER—HE WAS OF GREAT HELP TO PERRY ON MISSIONS.

HE COMMUNICATED WELL WITH THE JAPANESE BY WRITING ON PAPER, AS THERE WERE MANY WHO COULD READ AND WRITE CHINESE, EVEN THOUGH VERY FEW SPOKE IT.

IN JUNE 1853 THEY CONTINUED ON. IGNORING THE JAPANESE OFFICIALS' DEMANDS THAT THEY GO TO NAGASAKI, THEY HEADED INSTEAD FOR THE CAPITAL, EDO.

CHAPTER 2

AS THEY GOT CLOSER AND CLOSER
THE TENSION INCREASED ON ALL SIDES...

THEY STEAMED ALL THE WAY UP TO THE TOWN OF URAGA...
TURNING THE POWERFUL GUNS OF THE SHIPS TO FACE MENACINGLY TOWARD THE TOWN.
WE WILL NOT LEAVE, NOR GO TO NAGASAKI.
IF YOU ATTACK US, WE WILL TURN THE GUNS ON YOU, AND DESTROY YOUR TOWN.

WE GIVE YOU THIS
WHITE FLAG SO YOU CAN SHOW
US YOU SURRENDER···
GO BACK AND TELL
THAT TO YOUR SUPERIORS!

PERRY ORDERED THE SHIPS TO FIRE BLANK SHOTS FROM SEVENTY-THREE CANNONS...
BBUKKH
BBUKKH!
BBUKKH!
BUUUUKH!!!
HE CLAIMED IT WAS A CELEBRATION OF AMERICAN INDEPENDENCE DAY, BUT THE FEARSOME IMPRESSION IT MADE ON THE JAPANESE WAS SURELY NOT FAR FROM HIS MIND.

THE SIGN, WRITTEN IN FRENCH, READ: "WE ORDER YOU TO LEAVE IMMEDIATELY."

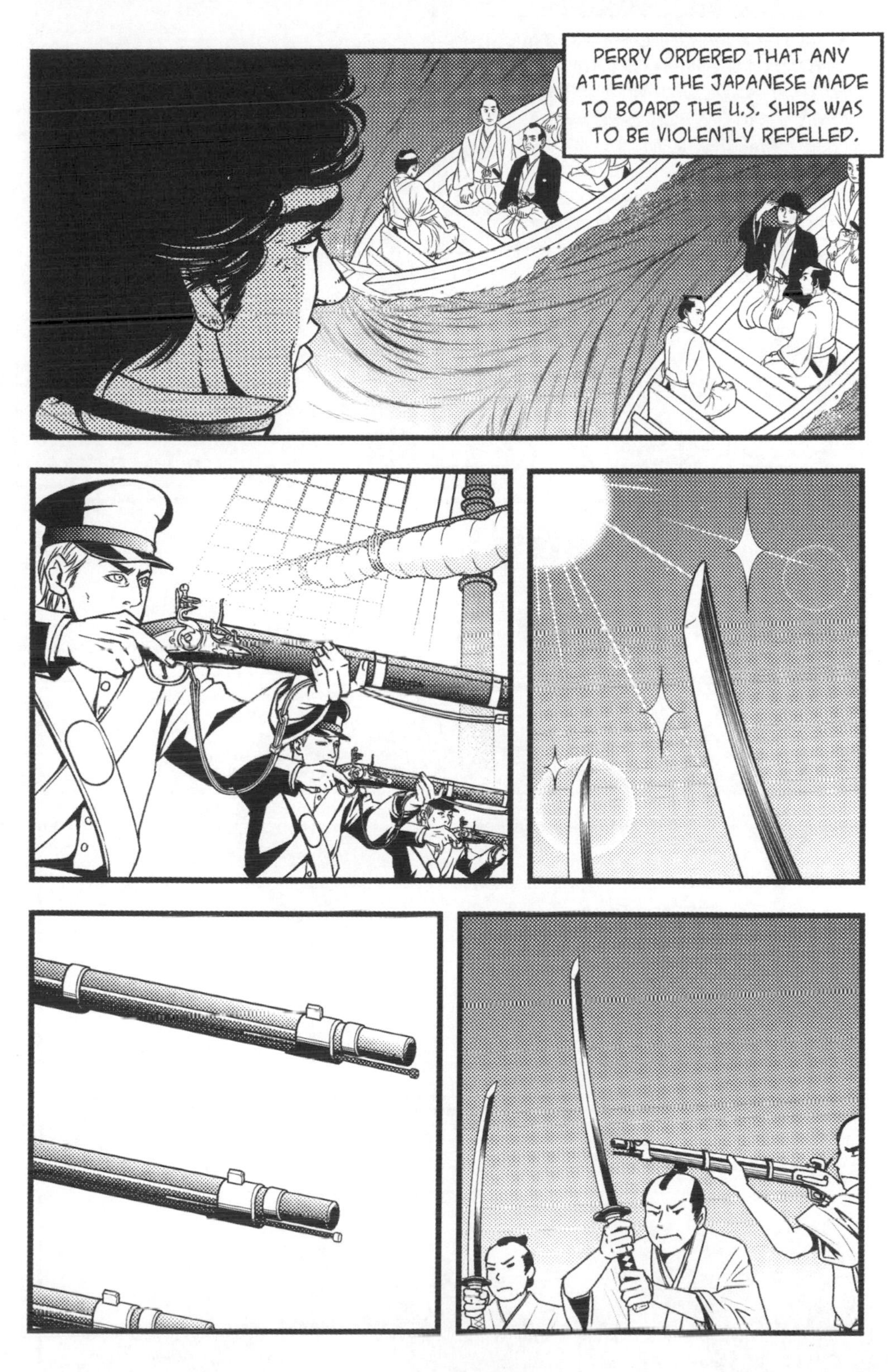
PERRY ORDERED THAT ANY ATTEMPT THE JAPANESE MADE TO BOARD THE U.S. SHIPS WAS TO BE VIOLENTLY REPELLED.

ON JULY 9 A MAN CALLED NAKAJIMA SABUROSUKE ROWED OUT TO THE *SUSQUEHANNA*, WITH NO GUARDS, ONLY AN INTERPRETER. HE WAS A YORIKI, A MIDDLE-RANKING MEMBER OF THE URAGA BUGYO, THE OFFICIAL ADMINISTORS OF THE URAGA AREA.
AT FIRST THE AMERICANS REFUSED TO ALLOW HIM ABOARD. BUT AFTER SOME NEGOTIATION, THEY ALLOWED HIM TO COME.
THESE ORDERS WILL MAKE IT CLEAR THAT NO FOREIGN SHIPS ARE ALLOWED INTO JAPANESE PORTS.
THANK YOU. I WILL SHOW THESE TO COMMODORE PERRY.*
*AS BEFORE, THESE TALKS ALSO TOOK PLACE FROM JAPANESE TO DUTCH TO ENGLISH AND BACK AGAIN.
TELL THEM I REFUSE TO TALK TO LOWER OFFICIALS.
I HAVE A LETTER FROM THE PRESIDENT OF THE UNITED STATES, AND ONLY HIGH-RANKING GOVERNMENT OFFICIALS WILL DO.
WHEN THE JAPANESE OFFICIALS HEARD THIS, THEY DECIDED TO SEND ANOTHER MAN TO PRETEND TO BE THE CHIEF OFFICIAL OF THE AREA.

THAT MAN, KAYAMA EIZAEMON, MET ANOTHER OFFICER, AS PERRY REFUSED TO MEET HIM TOO.
PLEASE TAKE YOUR SHIPS TO NAGASAKI...
THE DESIGNATED PORTS FOR FOREIGNERS.
WE HAVE HEARD THIS BEFORE, AND WE ARE GETTING RATHER SICK OF IT.
COMMODORE PERRY DEMANDS TO GIVE THE LETTER FROM THE PRESIDENT TO THE HIGHEST-RANKING OFFICIALS FROM EDO.
IF NOT, HE WILL MARCH TROOPS ON EDO—
AND DELIVER THE LETTER IN FORCE!

3日間
KAYAMA ASKED FOR THREE DAYS TO RESPOND.
THE REAL HEAD OFFICIAL OF THE URAGA BUGYO, IDO HIROMICHI, REPORTED THE SITUATION TO THE SHOGUN, WARNING THAT THEIR DEFENSES WERE NOT STRONG ENOUGH TO HOLD BACK THE AMERICANS IF THEY ATTACKED.
CRAAK!
IN THE MEANTIME, PERRY BEGAN A CAMPAIGN OF INTIMIDATION BY SENDING BOATS TO SURVEY THE SURROUNDING AREA, THREATENING TO USE FORCE IF THE JAPANESE GUARD BOATS AROUND THE AMERICAN SQUADRON DID NOT DISPERSE.

IN THE TENSE DAYS OF WAITING, THE AMERICANS PRACTICED THEIR COMBAT SKILLS, WELL AWARE THAT THE JAPANESE WERE WATCHING.
THIS ALSO GAVE WILLIAM HEINE, A GERMAN-BORN ARTIST WHO HAD ACCOMPANIED THE MISSION AND SKETCHED MANY PLACES AND SCENES IN 1853 AND 1854, TIME TO SKETCH.

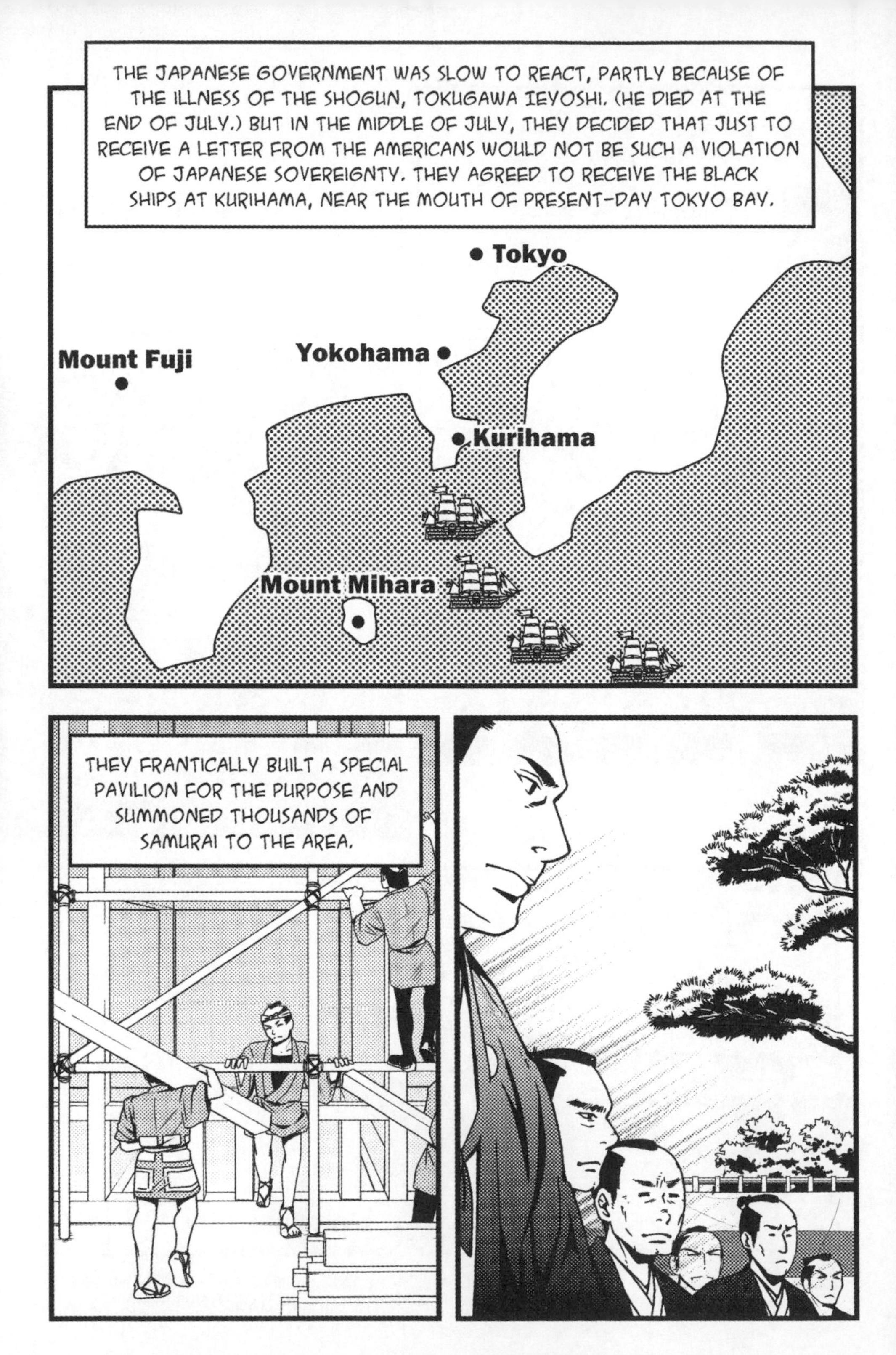
THE JAPANESE GOVERNMENT WAS SLOW TO REACT, PARTLY BECAUSE OF THE ILLNESS OF THE SHOGUN, TOKUGAWA IEYOSHI. (HE DIED AT THE END OF JULY.) BUT IN THE MIDDLE OF JULY, THEY DECIDED THAT JUST TO RECEIVE A LETTER FROM THE AMERICANS WOULD NOT BE SUCH A VIOLATION OF JAPANESE SOVEREIGNTY. THEY AGREED TO RECEIVE THE BLACK SHIPS AT KURIHAMA, NEAR THE MOUTH OF PRESENT-DAY TOKYO BAY.
Tokyo
Mount Fuji
Yokohama
Kurihama
Mount Mihara
THEY FRANTICALLY BUILT A SPECIAL PAVILION FOR THE PURPOSE AND SUMMONED THOUSANDS OF SAMURAI TO THE AREA.

THE SHIPS ARRIVED JULY 14, 1853.
Wa
Wa
Koff
Koff

ON THE SHORE, THOUSANDS OF SAMURAI WAITED, TENSE AND ARMED.

THE SHIPS WERE DRAWN UP SO THEIR GUNS COULD EASILY FIRE ASHORE, IF IT CAME TO THAT.

IS EVERYTHING READY, BUCHANAN?
ADAMS REPORTS THE BOATS ARE READY TO PUSH OFF, COMMODORE.
THEN LET'S BEGIN THIS LONG-AWAITED VENTURE.
SOUND THE SALUTE!
THERE WAS A THIRTEEN-GUN SALUTE FROM THE *SUSQUEHANNA*.
CREEEHH
CRREEHH

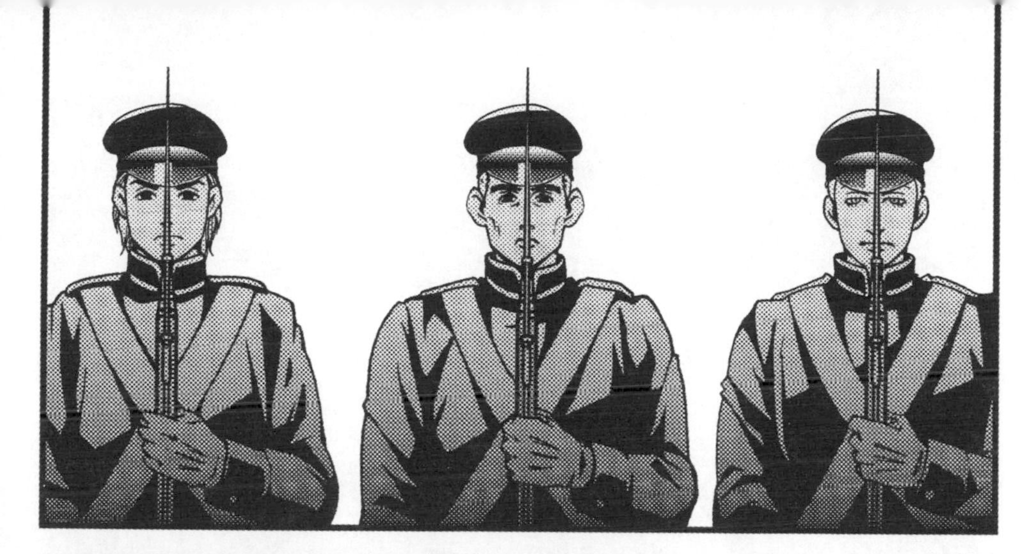

AS PERRY DESCENDED THE SHIP'S BAND PLAYED THE SONG "HAIL COLUMBIA."

'FIRM, UNITED LET US BE,
RALLYING ROUND OUR LIBERTY
AS A BAND OF BROTHERS JOINED,
PEACE AND SAFETY WE SHALL FIND.'

A SPECIAL AUDIENCE HALL OF WOOD AND CLOTH HAD BEEN BUILT. PERRY HANDED OVER THE OFFICIAL LETTER FROM PRESIDENT FILLMORE.
AGAIN, THE TALKS TOOK A LONG, DIFFICULT ROUTE FROM ENGLISH TO DUTCH TO JAPANESE AND BACK AGAIN··· WITH PERRY MAINTAINING HIS TOUGH STANCE.
WE DEMAND THE GOOD TREATMENT OF WHALERS IN JAPANESE WATERS AND THE PROTECTION OF STRANDED SAILORS.
YOU "DEMAND"?
YES. WE DO NOT ASK—
WE DEMAND.

TELL THEM THAT I CAN EASILY CALL ON FIFTY SHIPS SUCH AS THESE IN THE PACIFIC…
AND YET FIFTY MORE FROM CALIFORNIA.

THE SHIPS ARE FEARSOME MONSTERS.
BUT THEY CAN ONLY FIRE SO FAR.
WE CAN SIMPLY SIT AND WAIT, 10 PACES BEYOND THEIR RANGE.
QUITE WITHOUT TROUBLE.
PERHAPS.
BUT WE CAN DESTROY EVERYTHING WITHIN RANGE...
BAASSH!
AND WE CAN BLOCK YOUR SUPPLIES OF FOOD FROM REACHING EDO BY SEA. HOW LONG CAN YOUR PEOPLE SIT THAT OUT?

"AMERICANS HAVE ALSO BEEN APPALLED AT REPORTS THAT FOREIGNERS STRANDED IN JAPAN HAVE BEEN TREATED BADLY."
"OF THEM BEING SENT TO PLACES FAR FROM WHERE THEY LANDED, SQUASHED INTO SMALL PALANQUINS THAT DAMAGE THEIR LEGS."
WE ALSO DEMAND THE ESTABLISHMENT OF MUTUAL TRADE AGREEMENTS...
AND THE PROVISIONS OF COAL AND OTHER SUPPLIES AT ONE OR MORE PORTS.

THE MEETING WAS RELATIVELY BRIEF. PERRY LEFT WITH THE OMINOUS PROMISE TO RETURN IN APRIL OR MAY OF THE FOLLOWING YEAR.
THE JAPANESE KNEW THAT HE WOULD RETURN IN EVEN GREATER FORCE.

THE THREAT OF THE FOREIGNERS WAS REINFORCED WHEN PERRY, AGAINST THE WISHES OF THE SHOGUNATE, SAILED THE SHIPS FARTHER UP EDO BAY, SURVEYING THE COAST.

A SHORT WHILE LATER, THE
FOUR BLACK SHIPS LEFT JAPAN.

CHAPTER 3

AFTER THE SHIPS LEFT, THE SHOGUNATE POURED A LOT OF EFFORT INTO ITS COASTAL DEFENSES, ORDERING ALL THE CLANS IN COASTAL AREAS TO SET UP FORTS AND BATTERIES.
OVER THE COURSE OF THE YEAR THE TROUBLE THE BLACK SHIPS CAUSED AMONG MANY JAPANESE WAS ALSO EXPRESSED IN ARTISTIC FORMS, SUCH AS THIS ARMORED FISH PICTURE IN AN ESSAY COMPILED BY MOKITSU HACHIYA, A RETAINER OF THE TAYASU HOUSEHOLD.
IT SATIRIZED THE ATTEMPTS OF THE BAKUFU TO PROTECT THE COUNTRY AGAINST THE BLACK SHIPS. ITS DESIGN SUGGESTS A PLAY ON WORDS, ARMOR (BUGU) AND PUFFER FISH (FUGU). THREE CRESTS ARE DEPICTED SHOWING KEY CLANS INVOLVED IN DEFENSE: THE MATSUDAIRA OF THE KAWAGOE CLAN, THE MOURI OF THE CHOSHU CLAN, AND THE HOSOKAWA OF THE KUMAMOTO CLAN.

NORTH AMERICAN, PERRY

AND THIS FAMOUS KYOKA HUMOROUS POEM:
太平の
眠りを覚ます
上喜撰
たった四杯で
夜も眠れず
AWOKEN FROM SLEEP IN A PEACEFUL QUIET WORLD BY JOKISEN TEA; WITH ONLY FOUR CUPS OF IT, ONE CAN'T SLEEP, EVEN AT NIGHT.
OR WE MIGHT TRANSLATE IT IN A WAY THAT REVEALS THE HIDDEN MEANINGS MORE CLEARLY: "THE STEAM-POWERED SHIPS… BREAK THE HALCYON SLUMBER… OF THE PACIFIC… A MERE FOUR BOATS ARE ENOUGH… TO MAKE US LOSE SLEEP AT NIGHT."

A TRANSLATION OF PRESIDENT FILLMORE'S LETTER WAS SENT TO ALL THE MAJOR DAIMYO AND GOVERNMENT OFFICIALS.
RATHER THAN BEING SEEN AS A WISH TO INCLUDE VARIOUS INTERESTS, THIS WAS SEEN AS A SIGN OF WEAKNESS. REACTIONS WERE MIXED.
THE BAKUFU ARE WEAKLINGS. THEY LACK DECISIVENESS.
IT IS REQUESTED THAT YOU EXPRESS YOUR OPINIONS FREELY ON THE MATTER EVEN THOUGH THEY MAY BE CONTRARY TO ESTABLISHED POLICY.
WE SHOULD OPEN OUR DOORS, AT LEAST A LITTLE. LET US STUDY AND MASTER THE TECHNIQUES OF THE FOREIGNERS.
THEN PERHAPS LATER··· WE CAN TURN THE TABLES ON THEM.
I DISAGREE.
IF WE FAIL TO DRIVE THEM OFF NOW, WE SHALL NEVER HAVE ANOTHER CHANCE.

AFTER THE MEXICAN CESSION OF '48 WE HAVE BECOME A TRULY CONTINENTAL COUNTRY, BUCHANAN???EXPANDING RIGHT TO THE PACIFIC COAST, AS WAS OUR MANIFEST DESTINY.
LET ME QUOTE DIRECTLY FROM PRESIDENT ADAMS... NOW, WHERE IS THAT BOOK?
HERE IT IS.
LISTEN TO THIS, FROM AN 1811 LETTER TO HIS FATHER…
"THE WHOLE CONTINENT OF NORTH AMERICA APPEARS TO BE DESTINED BY DIVINE PROVIDENCE TO BE PEOPLED BY ONE NATION, SPEAKING ONE LANGUAGE, PROFESSING ONE GENERAL SYSTEM OF RELIGIOUS AND POLITICAL PRINCIPLES, AND ACCUSTOMED TO ONE GENERAL TENOR OF SOCIAL USAGES AND CUSTOMS..."
"FOR THE COMMON HAPPINESS OF THEM ALL, FOR THEIR PEACE AND PROSPERITY, I BELIEVE IT IS INDISPENSABLE THAT THEY SHOULD BE ASSOCIATED IN ONE FEDERAL UNION."

IT'S ONLY RIGHT AND PROPER THAT WE SHOULD CONTINUE WESTWARD EXPANSION ACROSS THE PACIFIC??? AND JAPAN IS ON THAT PATHWAY.
THERE, I FEAR, WE HAVE A DIFFERENCE, COMMODORE—I SEE AMERICA'S MORAL MISSION AS ONE OF DEMOCRATIC EXAMPLE RATHER THAN ONE OF CONQUEST.
AND IF EXAMPLE ALONE DOES NOT PROVE IMPRESSIVE ENOUGH, DO YOU SHIRK FROM THE USE OF FORCE?
NOT WHEN NECESSARY. I'VE SEEN BATTLE IN THE MEXICAN WAR.
OH, FORGIVE ME. I DID NOT MEAN TO QUESTION YOUR COURAGE.
I MEANT THAT THE OLIVE BRANCH OF PEACE MUST BE BACKED UP BY A BIG STICK. IF THE FIRST SETTLERS HAD LET THE NATIVE INDIANS PUSH THEM OUT OF VIRGINIA IN THE 1600S, THERE WOULD BE NO UNITED STATES NOW.

*HORACE GREELEY (1811-1872), EDITOR OF THE NEW YORK TRIBUNE, SPOKE THESE FAMOUS WORDS.

INDEED IT DID. MY FATHER'S FAMILY WOULD OFTEN SPEAK TO ME ABOUT THE BEAUTY OF SCOTLAND.
BUT MY COUNTRY NOW IS THE UNITED STATES OF AMERICA…
I DO NOT WANT THE IDEALS IT STANDS FOR TO BE REDUCED TO NOTHING MORE THAN THOSE OF A BULLY, RIDING ROUGHSHOD OVER WEAKER PEOPLES.
I TAKE IT, THEN, THAT YOU DO NOT SUBSCRIBE TO THE IDEA OF MANIFEST DESTINY?
I DO NOT, SIR. NAPOLEON ALSO THOUGHT HE HAD A DESTINY: TO DOMINATE EUROPE. AND LOOK WHAT HAPPENED TO HIM.
WELL, I APPRECIATE YOUR FRANKNESS.

WHEN WE RETURN TO JAPAN,
WE SHALL SEE...

FATHER!
WATCH ME!

YES, KOICHI. I'M WATCHING.
I WILL HIT THE BLACK SHIPS. WATCH THIS.
AHHH!
SPLOOSH
TRY AGAIN.
YEAAH!

WILL THE BLACK SHIPS COME BACK AGAIN, FATHER?
I WAS TOLD THEY WOULD COME BACK NEXT YEAR, KOICHI.
WILL YOU FIGHT THEM?
IF LORD HOSOKAWA COMMANDS US TO, YES.

DON'T WORRY.
COME ON— LET'S SEE IF I CAN HIT IT TOO.

BAAOOOMM!
MEANWHILE, THE AMERICANS PRACTICED THEIR SHOOTING SKILLS.
PUUUHH!

BAOMM!
A DIRECT HIT BOTH TIMES, THEN, SIR.
WELL DONE. EXCELLENT MARKSMANSHIP.

LATER IN 1853, PERRY AND HIS MEN ARRIVED BACK IN THE UNITED STATES. BUT THE RETURN TRIP WAS SOON ON THEIR MINDS.
WHEN IT'S TIME TO RETURN TO JAPAN, WE'LL BE READY TO TAKE ANY ACTION NECESSARY.
BUT DO YOU THINK IT WILL COME TO THAT, COMMODORE?
I'M REALLY OF TWO MINDS, BUCHANAN. THE JAPANESE WOULD BE FOOLISH TO FIGHT BACK.
AND YET I GET THE FEELING THAT MANY OF THEM WANT TO...
IT COULD GO EITHER WAY.

SOON PERRY LEARNED THAT A RUSSIAN SHIP, COMMANDED BY VICE ADMIRAL YEVFIMY PUTYATIN, HAD VISITED NAGASAKI SHORTLY AFTER THE AMERICAN BLACK SHIPS HAD LEFT JAPAN.

IT TOOK THE RUSSIANS A WHOLE MONTH OF DIFFICULT DISCUSSIONS UNTIL THE NAGASAKI BUGYO OFFICIALS FINALLY AGREED IN SEPTEMBER 1853 TO ACCEPT THE OFFICIAL LETTER PUTYATIN CARRIED FROM THE RUSSIAN FOREIGN MINISTER.
THE EXPEDITION WAS ACTUALLY MORE IMPRESSIVE THAN PERRY'S, BECAUSE IT INCLUDED SEVERAL EXPERTS ON CHINA, SCIENTISTS, ENGINEERS, AND A WELL-KNOWN AUTHOR, IVAN GONCHAROV.

WILL I HAVE A CHANCE TO GO ASHORE, ADMIRAL? I'M VERY KEEN TO STUDY THE JAPANESE WAY AND MANNERS.
THEY ARE BEING VERY SLOW AND DIFFICULT WITH US, GONCHAROV, MY DEAR FELLOW. BUT I'M HOPEFUL THAT YOU MAY YET GET THE OPPORTUNITY.

EVENTUALLY THEY WERE ALLOWED SHORE VISITS. ONE TIME A RUSSIAN ENGINEER, ALEXANDER MOZHAYSKY, DEMONSTRATED A STEAM ENGINE, WHICH WAS RELATIVELY NEW AT THAT TIME AND GREATLY IMPACTED INDUSTRY AND TRANSPORT.
SO, IF EACH ENGINE HAS ONE CYLINDER NINETY-FIVE INCHES IN DIAMETER, SUPPLIED WITH STEAM AT A PRESSURE OF SEVENTEEN POUNDS PER SQUARE INCH, IT CAN...
ONE OF THE MEN LISTENING WAS THE JAPANESE INVENTOR TANAKA HISASHIGE, WHO WAS MUCH INSPIRED BY THE DAY.
素晴らしい…
*WONDERFUL...
IT LATER LED TO HIM CREATE HIS OWN VERSIONS, WHICH POWERED JAPAN'S FIRST STEAM LOCOMOTIVE AND STEAM WARSHIP, THE *KANKO MARU*, IN 1855.

THE RUSSIANS SPENT A MONTH IN NAGASAKI TRYING TO NEGOTIATE A TREATY.
BUT THEY WERE UNSUCCESSFUL—THIS TIME!
INSTEAD, PUTYATIN DEPARTED TO SURVEY THE COASTS OF KOREA AND THE RUSSIAN FAR EAST TERRITORIES.
IN 1855 THE WRITER GONCHAROV PUBLISHED A HIGHLY INFLUENTIAL ACCOUNT OF HIS TRAVELS THROUGH AFRICA, JAPAN, AND ALASKA AND OF HIS JOURNEY BACK HOME THROUGH SIBERIA AND THE URAL MOUNTAINS.
JAPAN
INDONESIA

BACK IN THE UNITED STATES, PERRY WAS ALSO TOLD THAT THE BRITISH AND FRENCH INTENDED TO GO BACK TO JAPAN IN THE SPRING—SO THE AMERICANS DID NOT OBTAIN EXCLUSIVE PRIVILEGES.
THIS IS NOT GOOD NEWS. THE JAPANESE ARE BEING PRESSED FROM ALL SIDES BY OUR COMPETITORS.
WE NEED TO GET BACK AS SOON AS POSSIBLE???BEFORE THE WITHERING OF WINTER.
THEREFORE, TIME BEING TIGHT AND CIRCUMSTANCES TENSE, THE DECISION WAS MADE TO RETURN EARLIER THAN PLANNED.
PERRY AND HIS MEN RETURNED ON FEBRUARY 13, 1854, WITH A MUCH LARGER AND MORE POWERFUL FORCE—A TOTAL OF TEN VESSELS AND 1,600 MEN.

THE FLEET NOW INCLUDED THE SHIPS *LEXINGTON*, *MACEDONIAN*, *POWHATAN*, *VANDALIA*, *SOUTHAMPTON*, AND A SUPPLY SHIP.

CHAPTER 4

IN EDO, THE HEAD OF THE BAFUKU, ABE MASAHIRO, MEETS WITH OTHER IMPORTANT OFFICIALS.
EVERYONE HAS POINTED OUT THAT WE ARE WITHOUT A SIZEABLE NAVY AND OUR COASTS ARE POORLY DEFENDED.
MEANWHILE, THE AMERICANS WILL BE HERE AGAIN SOON.
OUR POLICY TOWARD THEM WILL BE TO EVADE ANY DEFINITE ANSWER, WHILE MAINTAINING A PEACEFUL STANCE.
IT MAY BE, HOWEVER, THAT VIOLENCE WILL ARISE.
SO WE MUST BE PREPARED IN ORDER TO AVOID DISGRACE.

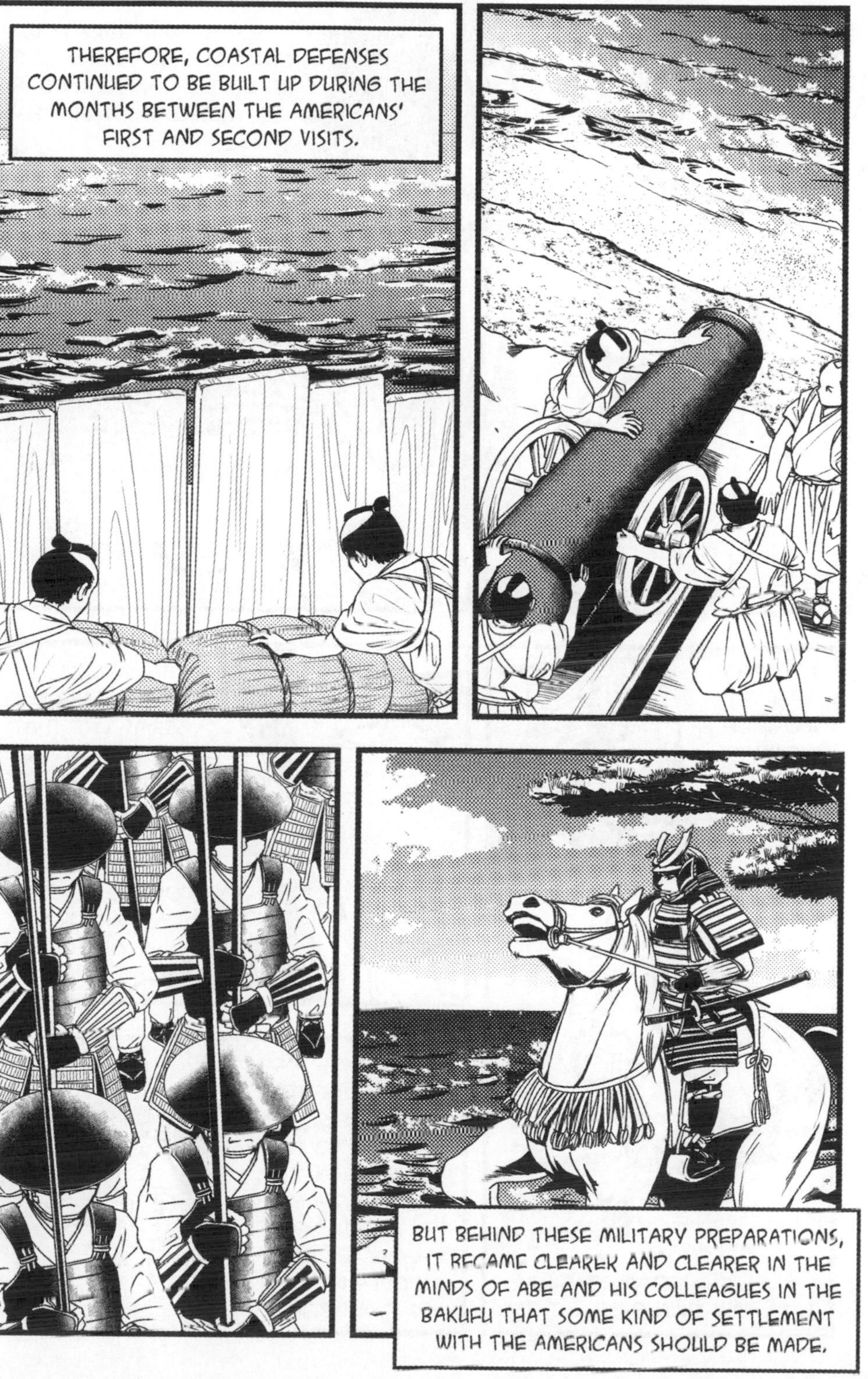
THEREFORE, COASTAL DEFENSES CONTINUED TO BE BUILT UP DURING THE MONTHS BETWEEN THE AMERICANS' FIRST AND SECOND VISITS.
BUT BEHIND THESE MILITARY PREPARATIONS, IT BECAME CLEARER AND CLEARER IN THE MINDS OF ABE AND HIS COLLEAGUES IN THE BAKUFU THAT SOME KIND OF SETTLEMENT WITH THE AMERICANS SHOULD BE MADE.

JAPAN
JAPANESE
JAPAN
SORRY TO DISTURB YOU, COMMODORE. WE WILL SOON REACH THE JAPANESE COAST, TO THE SOUTH OF EDO BAY.
THANK YOU, BUCHANAN. O'REILLY TOLD ME ALREADY.
I'VE BEEN READING MORE OF THE WATTS BOOK YOU GAVE ME.
THIS POINT CONFIRMS MY OWN OBSERVATIONS:
"THE CIVILIZATION OF THE JAPANESE SEEMS, LIKE THAT OF THE CHINESE, TO BE STATIONARY; BUT JAPAN HAS GERMS OF IMPROVEMENT WHICH OFFER SOME POSSIBLE PROSPECT OF A MORAL REVOLUTION."
"THE BRAVE AND INTELLIGENT JAPANESE COMES NEARER TO THE EUROPEAN, BY POSSESSING A MORE MASCULINE CHARACTER AND A HIGHER DEGREE OF CIVIL LIBERTY."

IS A MORAL REVOLUTION PART OF OUR MISSION, COMMODORE?
WHY, CERTAINLY.
MORALS AND MONEY... MORALS AND MONEY. I SEE NO CONTRADICTION BETWEEN THEM, DO YOU?
WELL, THE FRENCH IN THEIR REVOLUTIONARY PERIOD MAY NOT HAVE AGREED. AND THE BRITISH SOCIAL REFORMER ROBERT OWEN WROTE THAT AN EXCESS OF MONEY DAMAGES MORALS, AS DOES THE LACK OF IT.
THERE MAY BE SOMETHING TO WHAT HE SAYS. BUT I NOTE THAT OWEN'S NEW HARMONY SETTLEMENT IN INDIANA LASTED BUT TWO SHORT YEARS.
SUCH SOCIALIST AND UTOPIAN IDEAS ARE GOOD ON PAPER, BUT HAVE YET TO PROVE PRACTICAL.
SO FAR, YES. BUT SURELY FAILURE SO FAR DOES NOT MEAN SOMETHING IS FOREVER IMPOSSIBLE.
IF IT DOES, WHY ARE WE RETURNING TO JAPAN?

LISTEN...
KEH
KEH
KEH
KEH
KEH
KEH
KEH
KEH
KEH
IT'S THE FOUR BLACK SHIPS! THEY'RE BACK!

NO—THERE'S EVEN MORE!
EIGHT, NINE, TEN—I COUNT TEN OF THEM.
TEN!
WE'RE GOING TO NEED MORE GUNS.

BY THE TIME OF PERRY'S RETURN TO JAPAN, THE SHOGUNATE HAD DECIDED TO ACCEPT ALMOST ALL THE DEMANDS IN PRESIDENT FILLMORE'S LETTER. BUT THEY DISAGREED OVER THE SITE FOR NEGOTIATIONS—PERRY WANTED EDO, BUT THE JAPANESE SUGGESTED VARIOUS OTHER PLACES.
PERRY EVENTUALLY LOST HIS TEMPER…
YOU TELL THEM THIS: IF THEY DON'T AGREE TO A MEETING PLACE SOON, THEN WE WILL CALL ON A VAST INVASION FLEET—A HUNDRED SHIPS!
WE'LL MAKE WAR ON JAPAN!
THUUD!
ACTUALLY, A HUNDRED SHIPS WAS MORE THAN THE WHOLE U.S. NAVY AT THE TIME. BUT IT DIDN'T COME TO THAT, AS THEY COMPROMISED, AGREEING TO MEET AT WHAT WAS THEN THE TINY VILLAGE OF YOKOHAMA.
Tokyo
CHIBA
Yokohama
NORTH PACIFIC OCEAN
Kurihama
SHIZUOKA

WITH THREE DIFFERENT BANDS PLAYING "THE-STAR SPANGLED BANNER."

ON THE SHORE DIMLY SEEN

THROUGH THE MISTS OF THE DEEP...!

...WHERE THE FOE'S HAUGHTY
HOST IN DREAD SILENCE REPOSES
ONCE AGAIN, BOTH SIDES TRIED TO OVERAWE THE OTHER WITH A SHOW OF POWER.

THIS TIME THE NEGOTIATIONS WENT MORE SMOOTHLY, MOSTLY CARRIED OUT BY AKIRA HAYASHI, THE HEAD OF THE SHOHEIKO ACADEMY, WHICH WAS CONTROLLED BY THE SHOGUN.
IMPRESS ON HIM THAT THIS TIME, WE WILL NOT BE LEAVING UNTIL AN AGREEMENT IS SIGNED.
HE CAN SEE FOR HIMSELF THE SIZE OF THE FORCE WE HAVE WITH US. REMIND HIM THAT WE CAN DRAW ON FAR MORE.
PLEASE LET PERRY-SAMA KNOW THAT THE EXTENSIVE COASTAL DEFENSES WE HAVE BUILT SINCE HE WAS HERE ARE A TESTAMENT TO THE POWER WE KNEW HE WOULD RETURN WITH.
WE SAW SOMETHING OF THEM AS WE SURVEYED THE COAST. AND I HAVE ADMIRED THE TOUGHNESS AND VALOR OF YOUR FIGHTING MEN.
BUT BE IN NO DOUBT THAT OUR FAR LARGER SHIPS, MORE POWERFUL GUNS, AND SUPERIOR TECHNOLOGY WOULD TRIUMPH IN THE END.

AS NEGOTIATIONS MOVED ON, THE JAPANESE SIDE AGREED TO ALMOST ALL OF PERRY'S DEMANDS, EXCEPT THE TYPE OF COMMERCIAL AGREEMENTS THAT CHINA HAD BEEN FORCED INTO EARLIER.
THE TREATIES THAT YOUR GOVERNMENT AND THOSE OF SEVERAL OTHER WESTERN COUNTRIES SIGNED WITH CHINA ARE QUITE IMPOSSIBLE IN THE CASE OF JAPAN.
THE CHINESE MAY ALSO SOON HAVE CAUSE TO REGRET THOSE TREATIES THEMSELVES.
I AM PREPARED TO DELAY THE SIGNING OF AN EXTENSIVE COMMERCIAL TREATY???AS LONG AS OUR MAIN DEMANDS ARE MET.
THE MAIN PROBLEM WAS WHICH PORTS WOULD BE OPEN TO THE UNITED STATES. PERRY STRONGLY REJECTED NAGASAKI, AS THAT WOULD FEEL LIKE SIMPLY BEING LET INTO A PORT THAT WAS ALREADY HALF OPEN. HE WANTED NEW AND SIGNIFICANT PORTS OPENED TO THEM.

HAYASHI IS PLAYING A WEAK HAND VERY WELL.

INDEED. I THINK THE COMMODORE HAS MET HIS MATCH.

AFTER A RELATIVELY SHORT THREE WEEKS OF NEGOTIATIONS, THE TWO SIDES SIGNED THE CONVENTION OF KANAGAWA ON MARCH 31. IT WAS WRITTEN IN ENGLISH, DUTCH, CHINESE, AND JAPANESE.
HAKODATE
SHIMODA
THE PORTS OF SHIMODA AND HAKODATE WERE OPENED TO AMERICAN SHIPS, THOUGH THESE PLACES WERE NOT QUITE AS IMPORTANT AS THEY HAD HOPED FOR.
SHIPWRECKED SAILORS WOULD BE CARED FOR, AND AN AMERICAN CONSULATE WOULD BE ESTABLISHED AT SHIMODA.

AS CELEBRATORY PRESENTS, THE JAPANESE WERE GIVEN A MINIATURE STEAM LOCOMOTIVE, A TELEGRAPH APPARATUS, AGRICULTURAL TOOLS, CLOCKS, STOVES, BOOKS ABOUT THE UNITED STATES, AND ONE HUNDRED GALLONS OF WHISKEY!
THE JAPANESE GAVE THE AMERICANS GOLD-LACQUERED FURNITURE AND BOXES, BRONZE ORNAMENTS, PORCELAIN GOBLETS, AND A COLLECTION OF SEASHELLS, WHICH WAS A HOBBY OF PERRY'S.
THE SARATOGA LEFT FOR HOME WITH THE SIGNED TREATY, WHILE THE REST OF THE SQUADRON WENT TO SURVEY HAKODATE AND SHIMODA.

On the way home, Perry signed the compact between the United States and the Ryukyu Kingdom on July 11, 1854. Returning to the United States, he was made a rear admiral, and Congress awarded him $20,000. He published a report titled *Narrative of the Expedition of an American Squadron to the China Seas and Japan.*
On this second journey, Heine also made additional valuable sketches of life in Japan and of Yokohama, Shimoda, and Hakodate.
Meanwhile, the Russians were still hovering around Japan. Another Russian ship, the frigate *Diana*, arrived on July 11, 1854, with word that the Crimean War had broken out, putting Russia at war with France and Britain.
Soon the British Navy was hunting down the Russians at Nagasaki, so Putyatin decided to carry out his threat to sail for Edo itself, just as Perry had done. Meanwhile, the British began negotiating a treaty with Japan.

PUTYATIN ARRIVED AT SHIMODA ON NOVEMBER 22, 1854, AND STARTED NEGOTIATIONS THE FOLLOWING MONTH.
BUT THE DAY AFTER NEGOTIATIONS STARTED, A MAJOR EARTHQUAKE STRUCK.
RUMBBBLLEEE
GREESSSH!!!

ALL OF THE RUSSIAN SHIPS WERE DESTROYED APART FROM THE *DIANA*, WHICH WAS BADLY DAMAGED AND SANK SOON AFTERWARD. THE RUSSIANS WERE STRANDED IN JAPAN.

AN INTERESTING COUNTERFACTUAL: PERHAPS IF A TSUNAMI HAD COME EARLIER AND DESTROYED THE AMERICANS' SHIPS, THE JAPANESE MIGHT HAVE TAKEN THAT AS A SIGN THAT FORTUNE WAS ON THEIR SIDE AND BEEN ENCOURAGED TO REPEL THE FOREIGNERS.

THAT HAD HAPPENED BEFORE—THE MONGOL INVASION OF JAPAN BY KUBLAI KHAN IN THE LATE THIRTEENTH CENTURY WAS GREATLY WEAKENED BY TWO MASSIVE TYPHOONS THAT DESTROYED MOST OF THEIR SHIPS. THIS IS THE ORIGIN OF THE WORD KAMIKAZE ("DIVINE WIND").

BUT THIS TIME THE "DIVINE INTERVENTION" CAME TOO LITTLE, TOO LATE. AFTER HAVING AGREED TO THE AMERICANS, THERE PERHAPS SEEMED LITTLE POINT NOW IN REFUSING THE RUSSIANS, EVEN IN THEIR WEAKENED STATE. SO THE TREATY OF SHIMODA OF FEBRUARY 1855 OPENED THREE PORTS TO THE RUSSIANS AND FIXED THE BORDER OF JAPAN AND RUSSIA ON THE KURIL ISLANDS.

JAPAN HAD AT LEAST MANAGED TO AVOID THE ALMOST COMPLETE SUBJUGATION THAT CHINA HAD EXPERIENCED IN THE UNEQUAL TREATY SYSTEM. II NAOSUKE, THE DAIMYO OF HIKONE, WAS A KEY FIGURE WHO HAD RECOMMENDED THE ACCEPTANCE OF THE AMERICANS' TERMS.

CONDITIONS TODAY MEAN THAT IT IS IMPOSSIBLE TO ENSURE THE SAFETY OF OUR COUNTRY BY INSISTENCE ON SECLUSION.

WE MUST REVIVE THE TRADING VESSELS THAT EXISTED IN THE EARLY SEVENTEENTH CENTURY AND CONSTRUCT NEW STEAMSHIPS, ESPECIALLY POWERFUL WARSHIPS.

THIS IS THE BEST WAY OF BUILDING UP OUR STRENGTH SO THAT AT SOME POINT IN THE FUTURE WE MIGHT REIMPOSE THE BAN ON FOREIGNERS.

SINCE I UNDERSTAND THAT THE AMERICANS AND RUSSIANS HAVE ONLY RECENTLY BECOME SKILLED IN NAVIGATION, I DO NOT SEE HOW WE CLEVER AND QUICK-WITTED JAPANESE SHOULD PROVE INFERIOR TO THEM.

TWO YEARS LATER, IN 1856, TOWNSEND HARRIS WAS SENT TO BE THE AMERICAN CONSUL IN SHIMODA. HE MADE EVEN GREATER DEMANDS THAN PERRY'S AND REFUSED TO DELIVER HIS PRESIDENT'S LETTER TO ANYONE APART FROM THE SHOGUN IN EDO.
AFTER TWO TENSE YEARS OF NEGOTIATIONS, HARRIS AND TWO REPRESENTATIVES FROM II NAOSUKE (THEN THE TAIRO, GREAT ELDER, OF THE SHOGUNATE) SIGNED THE TREATY OF AMITY AND COMMERCE ON JULY 29, 1858.
IT OPENED THE PORTS OF KANAGAWA AND FOUR OTHER CITIES TO TRADE, ALLOWED FREEDOM OF RELIGIOUS EXPRESSION FOR FOREIGNERS, AND GRANTED EXTRATERRITORIALITY TO FOREIGNERS SO THEY WERE EXEMPTED FROM THE JURISDICTION OF JAPANESE
THE LAWS OF JAPAN ARE VERY PECULIAR, AND IT WOULD BE UNFAIR FOR FOREIGNERS TO LIVE UNDER SUCH RULES.
OF COURSE, MANY WERE ANGERED BY SUCH ATTITUDES AND THE TERMS OF THE TREATY. THE ENTRANCE OF FOREIGNERS TO EDO, THE CAPITAL OF THE SHOGUNATE, AND OF OFFICIALS FROM A FOREIGN GOVERNMENT NEAR THE EMPEROR WAS TOO MUCH FOR MANY.

SAKUMA SHOZAN, A MINOR OFFICIAL WITH THE BAKUFU, WAS ESPECIALLY CONCERNED ABOUT HOW TO REACT TO THE FOREIGNERS.
WHEN THE AMERICAN BARBARIANS ARRIVED IN THE BAY OF URAGA, THEIR MANNER WAS VERY ARROGANT AND AN INSULT TO OUR NATIONAL DIGNITY.
"AT THAT TIME A SAMURAI I KNOW SUFFERED THIS INSULT IN SILENCE..."
"BUT AFTER THE BARBARIANS HAD RETIRED, HE FIXED HIS GLARE AT A PORTRAIT OF PERRY THAT HAD BEEN LEFT AS A GIFT."
北亜墨利加人物
ペルリ像

Creeнннн!
"HE SLASHED THE PORTRAIT TO BITS!"
Riiipppp!

DESPITE HIS RESERVATIONS SAKUMA DECIDED THAT JAPAN SHOULD ADOPT WESTERN LEARNING AND TECHNOLOGY, BUT GROUND IT IN JAPANESE MORAL VALUES: "JAPANESE SPIRIT, WESTERN TECHNIQUE."
HE ROSE IN THE RANKS OF THE BAKUFU AS THEY STRUGGLED TO FIND PEOPLE WHO COULD DEAL WITH THE NEW SITUATION. BUT, AS HAS HAPPENED AT SEVERAL POINTS IN JAPANESE HISTORY, RADICAL EXTREMISTS DAMNED HIS POSITION.
YaaaAHH!!
SliKKK
IN AUGUST 1864, SAKUMA WAS MURDERED IN BROAD DAYLIGHT BY AN ADHERENT OF THE SONNO JOI SCHOOL.

THE SONNO JOI SCHOOL'S ROUSING CRY "REVERE THE KING, EXPEL THE BARBARIANS" WAS ADOPTED BY THE REBELLIOUS PROVINCES, ESPECIALLY CHOSHU AND SATSUMA, AND FOCUSED RESISTANCE ON THE TREATY OF KANAGAWA.

THE EMPEROR KOMEI HAD SOME SYMPATHY WITH THIS, AND BREAKING WITH CENTURIES OF IMPERIAL TRADITION, HE BEGAN TO TAKE AN ACTIVE ROLE IN THE GOVERNMENT OF JAPAN AND INTERFERE MORE WITH THE SHOGUNATE'S BUSINESS.

THIS CULMINATED IN MARCH 1863 WITH THE ORDER TO EXPEL BARBARIANS. THOUGH THE SHOGUNATE SIDELINED THIS ORDER, IT FURTHERED INSPIRED ATTACKS AGAINST FOREIGNERS AND THE SHOGUNATE ITSELF.

FOR EXAMPLE, THE ENGLISH TRADER CHARLES LENOX RICHARDSON WAS RETIRING FROM HIS SUCCESSFUL BUSINESS IN CHINA AND DECIDED TO TAKE A TRIP TO JAPAN BEFORE RETURNING HOME TO BRITAIN.

OH, LOOK AT THAT.
WHAT?
GET AWAY FROM LORD SHIMAZU!
NEH!
OH, GOD!
CLIP
CHARLES!
OH, BLOODY HELL!
CLOP!
OOHHF!

KILL HIM.
NO, WAIT! HE MEANT NO HARM!
SLiiCCK
aaah!

FOLLOWING THE MURDER OF RICHARDSON, THE OUTRAGED BRITISH GOVERNMENT DEMANDED A STERN REPARATION OF £100,000, ROUGHLY A THIRD OF THE TOTAL YEARLY REVENUES OF THE BAKUFU. OTHERWISE, THEY WOULD BOMBARD EDO!

THEY ALSO DEMANDED THAT THE SATSUMA DOMAIN, WHERE SHIMUZU WAS FROM, SHOULD ARREST THE MEN WHO CARRIED OUT THE ATTACK AND PAY £25,000 COMPENSATION TO THE RELATIVES OF RICHARDSON AND THE SURVIVORS.

ANOTHER SYMBOLIC SCENE OF INSURGENCY WAS THE ASSASSINATION OF II NAOSUKE IN 1860 FOR HIS PART IN SIGNING THE TREATY OF AMITY AND COMMERCE WITH THE UNITED STATES.
YAAGHHH!!
SLLiiCCK!
THAT SUCH AN IMPORTANT OFFICIAL COULD BE CUT DOWN DEAD AT THE VERY GATES OF THE SHOGUN'S EDO CASTLE COULD BE SEEN AS A SIGN THAT THE SHOGUNATE WAS NO LONGER IN CONTROL.

IN THE TWO DECADES SINCE THE BLACK SHIPS ARRIVED, JAPAN'S COURSE HAD CHANGED DRAMATICALLY—AND WOULD CONTINUE TO SHIFT AS THE END OF THE SHOGUNATE LOOMED.

THE END.

ABOUT THE AUTHOR AND ILLUSTRATOR

Photo by Asahi Shinbun

SEAN MICHAEL WILSON is a Harvey- and Eiser-award-nominated comic book writer who has authored more than a dozen graphic novels and manga comics, including adaptations of *The Book of Five Rings* and *The 47 Ronin.* He is also the editor of the critically acclaimed anthology *AX: A Collection of Alternative Manga* (one of Publishers Weekly's "Best Ten Books of 2010"). Originally from Scotland, he now lives in Japan.

AKIKO SHIMOJIMA is a comic and manga artist from Tokyo, Japan. A teacher of digital comics art at a school in Tokyo, she is the illustrator of *The 47 Ronin* and has contributed work to many other publications. Her previous book with Sean Michael Wilson, *The Secrets of the Ninja,* won an Honorary Mention in the 10th Annual International Manga Awards.

TITLES BY SEAN MICHAEL WILSON AND AKIKO SHIMOJIMA

available from North Atlantic Books

Secrets of the Ninja

978-1-58394-864-4